THE POWER OF SPORTSMANSHIP

Featuring the story of Jim Thorpe

Della Mae Rasmussen
Phyllis Colonna

Art Illustrator
Stephen P. Krause

Editor, Layout and Research
Beatrice W. Friel

THE POWER OF SPORTSMANSHIP

Featuring the story of Jim Thorpe

Advisors
Paul and Millie Cheesman
Mark Ray Davis
Rodney L. Mann, Jr.
Roxanne Shallenberger
Dale T. Tingey

Publisher
Steven R. Shallenberger

Director and Correlator
Lael J. Woodbury

AN EAGLE SYSTEMS
INTERNATIONAL
PUBLICATION
ANTIOCH, CALIFORNIA

The Power of Sportsmanship
Copyright © 1981 by
Power Tales
Eagle Systems International
P.O. Box 1229
Antioch, California 94509

ISBN: 0-911712-94-1

Library of Congress Catalog No.: 81-50868

First Edition

Lithographed in USA by
COMMUNITY PRESS, INC.

A member of
The American Bookseller's Association
New York, New York

Dedicated to young sports lovers in the hopes that they will keep the rules of good sportsmanship and strive to be cheerful winners and courteous losers.

JIM THORPE

Jim Thorpe was born in 1888 in a cabin near the North Canadian River on the Sac and Fox Indian Reserve in northern Oklahoma. His father, Hiram, the son of an Indian woman and an Irishman, was brought up on the Sac and Fox reserve in Kansas. His mother, Charlotte Vieux, had a French father and an Indian mother with both Potawatomi and Kickapoo blood. She bore eleven children.

Jim had a twin brother, Charles. Their childhood was spent in the wilderness area of the reservation. They picked wild plums, grapes, and pecans and learned to set traps for small game. When Jim was about eight, he brought down his first deer.

But life was not always easy. The family had to cope with drought and flies in summer and bitter cold spells in winter. With the rush of white settlers to Indian territory came rustlers, who often slaughtered cattle and hogs, taking the meat they wanted and leaving the rest on the ground to spoil. Horse thieves were also a problem.

The twins were enrolled in the Sac and Fox mission school at the age of six. The school was a manual labor boarding school. It took the children away from their home and placed them under a regimen of tight discipline, simple labor, and part-time study. School life here was regimented and much different than the carefree life of the reservation the children were use to.

Jim was quick for his age and could use his legs better than most of his companions in their favorite tests of strength, such as scuffling and wrestling. He didn't like school. Charles was remembered as having been a "sweet and gentle" pupil, while Jim was said to have been "boisterous and restless." When the twins were about ten, Charles died of pneumonia, leaving a lonely and confused twin brother.

After Charles's death Jim ran away from school. He was then enrolled at Haskell Institute, which was about 300 miles from home. At Haskell he learned to play football, using a stocking stuffed with rags and grass for a ball. Here he also played baseball.

When he was about fourteen Jim left Haskell because of illness in the family. His father had been wounded in a hunting accident. A short time later his mother died from complications of childbirth. While at home, Jim attended a nearby school and helped out with the younger children.

In February 1904 Jim, now sixteen, enrolled at Carlisle, an Indian school in Pennsylvania. He had only been there a short time when his father died.

Jim first became known in sports in 1907, when he won the school 120-yard hurdles, the high jump, and took second in the 220-yard dash. In baseball and football his coach said he was a good learner, was quick to do things the way he was taught, and wasn't afraid.

With his success in sports, Jim's academics improved. He left Carlisle for two years to play baseball in the Rocky Mount League. In 1911 he returned to Carlisle.

He was named all-American halfback in 1911 and 1912. At the 1912 Olympics in Sweden he won the pentathlon and decathlon events (the only time this was ever done by one individual).

From 1913 to 1919 Jim played major league baseball, and he was an outstanding professional football player from 1920 to 1926. He was considered by many to be the finest all-around athlete in history. He not only excelled in football, track, and baseball, but he was also very good at lacrosse, bowling, golf, and other sports.

Jim was married three times and was the father of three daughters and five sons. He died of a heart attack on 28 March 1953 in his Lomita, California, trailer home.

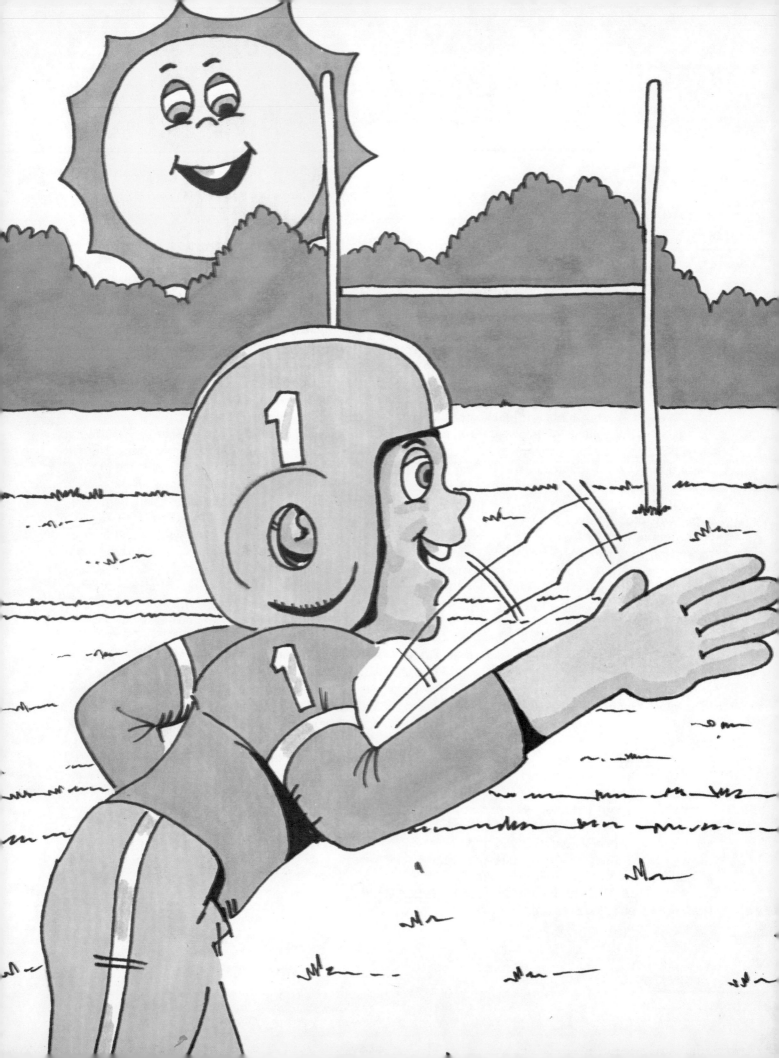

Robbie threw the football with all his strength. It spiraled right into the waiting hands of his best friend, Jason.

"Not too bad!" Jason called. "Another perfect pass! Are you practicing to be the world's greatest athlete?"

"Of course!" Robbie said, laughing. "Just call me Jim Thorpe."

The two boys had been playing hard, and now it was time to go home. They started toward the empty school to change clothes and put their gear away.

7

"Who's Jim Thorpe?" Jason asked. His black hair was tousled from the football helmet and his eyes were such a deep brown they almost seemed black.

"Who's Jim Thorpe?" Robbie asked in disbelief. "You've got to be kidding! He's only the greatest football player that ever lived, that's all! In fact, he's probably one of the greatest sportsmen that ever lived. He was good at everything he ever tried!"

Robbie's hair was as red and curly as Jason's was black and straight. His short nose was sprinkled with freckles from the hot summer sun. The two boys had been best friends since Robbie moved to Jason's school in the third grade. That was two years ago.

"Well, I've never heard of him before, and I know all the best players in pro football," Jason answered. "What team is he on?"

"He's not on any team," Robbie said. "He was a big hero when my grandpa was growing up. We have an autographed picture of him at home. He played for Carlisle."

"Carlisle!" Jason laughed. "Is this a joke? I've never heard of Carlisle either. What is it, a junior high school?"

"Carlisle was a school for Indians," Robbie answered coldly. "It was where Jim Thorpe went to school, and it's where my grandpa went to school. You want to make something of it?"

"Here now—what's going on down there?" a voice boomed out above them. The two boys jumped and stared around the empty locker room.

"I thought we were alone," Jason whispered.

"We *are* alone," Robbie whispered back.

"Oh no you're not. You're just not looking in the right place," the voice boomed out again. It came from the top shelf of the trophy cabinet against the wall.

"A talking trophy!" Jason gasped, his brown eyes opening wide. "This is ridiculous!"

"No more ridiculous than two best friends having a big fight over sportsmanship," the trophy said sternly. "Now what's this argument all about?"

Robbie gulped. "I was just telling Jason about Jim Thorpe—about him being one of the greatest sportsmen who ever lived," he began.

"And I was just telling Robbie that I've never heard of Jim Thorpe—or the school he played for," Jason finished. "How can he be such a great sportsman if nobody has ever heard of him?"

"Just because you've never heard of him doesn't mean everybody else hasn't heard of him," Robbie said.

"Now, now—that's enough!" the trophy said firmly. "Since this is an argument about sportsmanship, what do you think is a fair way to settle it?"

The two boys stared at each other, but neither one could think of a good idea.

"Don't you think the fairest way is to get the facts and let Jason decide for himself?" the trophy asked.

15

"But where will we get the facts?" Jason asked.

"I'm going to give them to you," the trophy said happily. He climbed down to the middle shelf, where the boys could see him better and where he could keep an eye on them, too.

"Pull that mat over here and get comfortable," he said. "It takes more than five minutes to tell about a man like Jim Thorpe."

Jason and Robbie pulled the mat close to the cabinet and sat down cross-legged to hear the trophy's story.

"Jim was born in Oklahoma Territory just after sunrise on the morning of May 28, 1888," he began. "His mother was a Potawatomi Indian named Charlotte, and it was the custom of her people to name a baby after something that happened at the time of his birth.

"Charlotte looked out the window and saw the rising sun shining on the path to the door of her cabin. She said to her baby, *"I will give you the Indian name of Wo-tho-huck. That means Bright Path."*

"That was a good name!" Robbie said.

"Yes, that was a good name," the trophy answered. "This baby's path would someday be bright in the world of sports, when everyone but his Indian friends would come to know him by the name Jim Thorpe."

"Was Jim's father Indian, too?" Jason asked. "What was his name?"

"Jim's father was part Indian," the trophy answered. "His name was Hiram Thorpe. Hiram's mother was from the Thunder Clan of the famous warrior, Chief Black Hawk. But his father was an Irish trapper with a strong body and a big mustache. He was also named Hiram Thorpe."

"Many people say Jim's father was a direct descendant of Chief Black Hawk," the trophy continued. "Tribesmen in the Thunder Clan said he looked just like the famous chief. They said he was like Black Hawk in many other ways, too. He was the great athlete in the tribe. Whenever the Indians had contests of speed, skill, or endurance, Jim's father won."

"Jim's father was a good hunter, too. He could track buffalo for many days and nights, or he could bring down a small bird with only one shot. One day when he was a long way from camp, he shot two large deer. He didn't have a horse, so he threw a deer across each shoulder and carried them for twenty miles."

"Jim's father must have been strong!" Robbie said.

"He was strong," the trophy answered. "He taught his sons to be strong, too. Jim had an older brother, George, and a twin brother named Charlie. His father told them, *"If boys want to grow up to be strong men, they have to work hard and play hard when they are young."*

"He taught his sons to hunt and fish and track wild animals. They spent almost all of their time outdoors, summers and winters. Sometimes they held contests to prove their skill. They swam rivers, climbed tall cedar trees, or jumped on the backs of wild horses to see who was the fastest or the strongest.

"But the most important thing Jim's father taught them was to keep the rules of good sportsmanship. He taught them to try to win with the best that was in them, but never to hold a grudge or to be a poor sport when they lost."

"I didn't know Jim Thorpe had a twin brother," Robbie interrupted. "Did they look exactly alike?"

"No, they weren't look-alike twins," the trophy answered. "As a matter of fact, Jim looked like his father and Chief Black Hawk, while Charlie looked more like his Irish grandfather, Hiram. The two boys were best friends as well as twin brothers from the time they were born. But just before their tenth birthday a terrible thing happened. Charlie became very sick with pneumonia. In less than a week he died."

"For nearly ten years the two brothers had roamed the prairies and swam and played together. Now Jim felt alone and very sad. Often he would go out into the wilderness with only his dog for company. Sometimes he would make a camp and stay all night."

"George was seven years older than Jim, but he was worried about his brother. He began to include him in his work and play. Soon he and Jim were as close as Jim and Charlie had been."

"This was good for Jim because he had to work twice as hard to keep up with his older brother, and this made him an even stronger sportsman. The boys became powerful swimmers and runners. When they went hunting with their father, they needed all the strength and endurance they had developed. He often walked thirty miles in one day, then made a camp before he rested."

"Their father was very popular with the other Indian families. Once a week everyone gathered in a big field by the Thorpe home. They all brought food for an evening feast, then spent the day competing in athletic contests. They had running, jumping, swimming, wrestling, and horseback-riding contests. Whatever Jim's father entered, he won. The other men of the tribe laughed. *"We shouldn't even bother to play against you,"* they told him."

"We know you will win before we start." But they didn't mind because they knew that Hiram Thorpe was their true friend. He believed that all men were brothers and should be treated with respect. He taught Jim and George to believe that, too. Whether they won a contest or lost it, they played with good humor and sincere friendship."

29

"Jim had work to do, too. His father owned more than 300 acres of land, and it was Jim's job to feed all the livestock and do other chores. He was especially good at catching and taming wild horses. He fished and hunted for food for the family, but he never killed more than they needed to eat. He believed in sportsmanship with animals as well as people. He was a careful marksman, and he always shot an animal cleanly so it wouldn't suffer or run away wounded."

THINK ABOUT IT

1. Can you name three ways Jim's father taught him the rules of good sportsmanship?
2. Can you think of three ways Jim and his brothers built strong, athletic bodies?

30

"Didn't Jim ever have to go to school?" Jason asked. "I wish I could spend all my time swimming and fishing or riding horses."

"Oh yes, Jim had to go to school," the trophy said, chuckling. "When he was only six years old he went to a boarding school twenty-three miles from his home. He went with George and Charlie, and he didn't like it at all. You see, the Indian children spoke the language of their tribe, but all the school books were written in English. Besides learning how to read and write, they had to learn another language."

"Charlie was quite good at his studies—at least it didn't bother him to work at his desk all day. But Jim longed to be outside. The only subject he liked was baseball. So long as Charlie was alive, Jim tried to make the best of school. But after Charlie died, he felt he couldn't stay there any longer. It was too full of sad memories. Jim decided to run away and go home."

"He walked all day, more excited with every passing mile at the thought of being with his family again. But when he saw the stern look on his mother's face, he thought perhaps he had made a bad decision."

"His father looked even more stern than his mother. He hitched up the horse and wagon and drove Jim right back to school again. But as soon as his father left by the front door, Jim slipped out the back door. He knew a shortcut home that was only eighteen miles long instead of twenty-three. He was only ten years old, but he ran the whole eighteen miles. When his dad arrived in the wagon, Jim was already waiting for him. Mr. Thorpe could hardly believe his eyes."

"When Mr. Thorpe understood how hard that school was for Jim, especially with so many sad memories of Charlie, he decided to send his son to a new school. He chose Haskell in Kansas. Haskell was a school especially for Indians, and it was far enough away that he didn't think Jim would try to walk home again."

"Jim knew his father wanted what was best for him, so he gave in like the good sport that he was. Besides, he liked this school much better. The teachers were interesting and kind, and it was at Haskell that Jim first learned to play football. From the first time he saw football, he was fascinated by it, and he learned everything he could about it."

"The year Jim turned about fourteen, his mother suddenly died. Jim had no heart to return to school so far away. He worked for a year on a ranch and then he began school at Garden Grove, only three miles from his home. He was able to help with the chores after classes, and he could help his father take care of his sister Mary, who was eight, and his brother Eddie, who was three."

"Jim still liked sports; whenever he had free time he played baseball. The team he played on became well-known throughout Oklahoma. Everyone said Jim could outplay anyone with either hand in any spot on the diamond. In fact, his fame in all kinds of sports spread all the way to a man named Pop Warner."

"Glen S. 'Pop' Warner was one of football's greatest coaches. He had made Carlisle Indian School in Pennsylvania known throughout all the country for its great sportsmen—and especially its great football players.

"Pop Warner had heard about Jim's abilities as an athlete. One day a man in a blue uniform came to talk to Jim at his school. *"I am from Carlisle,"* the man said. *"I have come to see if you will attend our school."*

"Carlisle! All the Indians knew that name. It was a name they were proud of. Pop Warner had made it famous in the sports world. By this time Jim was very serious about his education as well as sports, and Carlisle was the best Indian school there was. He went to talk to his father and his father urged him to go. To be asked to attend Carlisle was a great honor. *"You are an Indian, Jim. Go show other people what we can do,"* his father said."

"When he arrived at Carlisle, Jim was sixteen years old. The school had once been the headquarters of General George Washington, and it was still very military. The oldest buildings were brick barracks built by the soldiers during the American Revolution.

"All the boys wore blue cavalry uniforms. Their shoes had to be shined at all times. Every morning at six o'clock a bugle signaled that it was time to get up. At nine o'clock at night it signaled time to go to bed. The boys enjoyed the military discipline. Every Saturday there was an inspection, and often competitive drills were held on the parade grounds."

"Jim studied half of every school day, then he worked at a chosen trade for a half day. But his great love was sports."

"Was Jim big for his age?" Jason asked.

"No, as a matter of fact, he wasn't," the trophy answered. "When he was sixteen, he was only 5 feet 5 1/2 inches tall and weighed 115 pounds. At first it was hard for him to make the coaches believe he could be good at sports when most of the other players were so much taller and heavier."

"One day Jim was watching the track team practice the high jump. It was Saturday and Jim was wearing overalls, an old shirt, and gym shoes he had borrowed from someone else. *"Will you let me try one jump?"* he asked when the bar was so high that no one else could clear it.

"The tall track stars laughed at the new boy. *"Sure,"* they said. *"Try it where it is."* Jim sailed over the bar with a half inch to spare. The track team was astonished, and now it was Jim's turn to laugh."

"Next day Pop Warner called him into his office. "Do you know what you've done?" he asked.

"Nothing bad, I hope," Jim answered.

"Bad!" Pop answered. "Boy, you've just broken the school record for the high jump."

"I think I could do even better in a track suit," Jim answered."

"Pop sent him a suit and made him a member of the track team. That spring Jim broke the track and field records of the school meet.

"But Pop still wasn't convinced Jim was strong and big enough to play football. *"He may be a track star,"* the coach thought, *"but he isn't football material. Football is for big guys."*

"Jim wouldn't leave Pop alone. *"I want to play football,"* he said.

"Come back when you gain weight," Pop told him. *"You're too skinny— you'd get killed."*

"But Jim wouldn't go away. He found an old tattered football suit. It was full of holes and much too big. When Jim trotted out onto the field, Pop yelled, *"What are you doing here?"*

"I want to play football! Jim answered."

"Maybe he needs to be taught a lesson," Pop thought to himself. He threw Jim a football and sent him out onto the field. *"Give the varsity some tackling practice,"* he said.

"He thought Jim would be out of the game in the first half minute, but he had a surprise in store. Jim ran down the field with such speed and power

that no one could touch him. He plowed through the big tacklers as if they were butter. Pop Warner stood on the sidelines with his mouth open.

"Jim was made a member of the varsity team. However he didn't play much that year. Pop wanted him to learn the game thoroughly first."

THINK ABOUT IT

1. Why do you think Carlisle Indian School had such good athletes?
2. How do you think the games Jim played when he was young helped him to be a good football player?

JIM REACHES THE TOP

"By 1908, when Jim was twenty, he had almost reached his full growth. One friend who hadn't seen him for a long time said, "Jim you've grown as big as a mule." That fall Coach Warner said, "I think you're ready for football."

"I'll bet he *was* ready, too!" Robbie said.

The trophy chuckled. "He was Robbie—he was indeed. In his first game he stunned the crowd with five touchdowns from the far end of the field, and he threw for another score on a 30-yard pass. And that was only the first half!"

"In the next game the score was tied nothing-to-nothing in the second half. It was played at Carlisle, and the crowd was screaming, *"We want Jim! We want Jim!"* Finally Pop Warner tapped him on the shoulder, and Jim went in. He blasted into the line with the loudest crash you ever heard. For seventy yards the opposing team tried to bring him down, but they couldn't. He just kept yelling, *"Out of my way—get out of my way."* The crowd loved him."

"Jim played for Carlisle for several years, and soon every newspaper in the country was writing about him. Pop Warner told one reporter, *"No college player has ever had the natural skill for sports that Jim has. He can penetrate a line and see holes to break through in a second. He runs with dazzling speed. He can go farther with a tackler hanging onto him than any man I ever knew. He concentrates; he sizes up a situation quickly. He is the same in every sport."* The newspapers began to write, *"Jim Thorpe is the most versatile athlete ever known."*

"In 1912 Jim was elected captain of the football team. That year Carlisle won eleven games and lost one. They had 298 points to 49 for the opposition.

"But an even greater honor came to Jim. He was chosen to participate in the Olympic Games in Stockholm, Sweden. The U.S. Olympic Team sailed on June 14, 1912, and for nine days their ship echoed with the sound of pounding feet. All the way across the Atlantic Ocean the Olympic runners ran around and around the deck to keep in shape, and leading them all was Jim Thorpe."

"From the beginning of the Olympic games, America's team was way ahead. In fact, the 1912 games were recorded in history as 'The Olympics of Jim Thorpe.' In the pentathlon he won the broad jump and was second in the javelin throw. He also won the 200-meter dash, the discus throw, and the 1500-meter race. When the points were figured, his score was three times higher than the score in second place. Everyone was amazed. His performance still hasn't been equaled today."

"But he didn't stop there. At the end of the decathlon he had a score of 8,412 points out of 10,000 possible. He was 700 points ahead of the man in second place."

"When the games were over, King Gustav of Sweden presented the medals and trophies to Jim. The crowd and Jim's fellow athletes cheered. The king took Jim's hand in his own and said, *"Sir, you are the greatest athlete in the world."* It was the proudest moment of Jim's life. *"Thanks, King,"* he said softly. In competition Jim was fierce and determined; but off the field he was gentle, kind, and modest."

"When he returned to America, bands played and crowds cheered wherever he went. One speaker told him, *"You have covered yourself with glory. You have brought honor to your country. You inspire people to live cleaner, healthier, more vigorous lives."*

"Was that the end of his fame?" Jason asked.

"Oh no," the trophy answered. "Jim went from honor to honor in the sports world. He played football for one more year at Carlisle. In fact, in one game he played against a man who would later become President of the United States. Dwight D. Eisenhower was playing for Army the day Carlisle beat Army 27 to 6."

"Jim became a professional baseball player and a professional football player after leaving Carlisle, but all his life he was good at every sport. He could play any position in basketball, and he was a powerful swimmer. He could win at golf, tennis, or bowling. When he was sixty years old, he was still running races!"

58

"In his last years Jim liked to take part in school assemblies all over America. He always walked on stage in a big Indian headdress. He would tell the students about his life—especially about when he was a young boy growing up on the reservation. He would tell them about his love of sports and good sportsmanship and how important they had been in his life."

"In 1951 Hollywood made a movie called *Jim Thorpe—All-American*. He was named best athlete in the first half of the 20th century. In 1975, twenty years after Jim died, he was elected to the National Track and Field Hall of Fame. In 1977 he was named the greatest American football player in history. In fact, a football trophy was named for him. Every year the Jim Thorpe Trophy is given to the most valuable player in the National Football League."

"I guess maybe Jim Thorpe *was* one of the greatest athletes that ever lived," Jason said.

"Well, he was a great athlete, but he wasn't only an athlete, Jason—he was a man who truly believed in sportsmanship. No one ever heard Jim say bad things about other people. His friendship and his big smile were as famous as his wins and his trophies. Even when other players broke the rules, Jim wouldn't. And win or lose, he always ran over with a hug or a warm handsake for the man who was playing against him."

"I guess I wasn't very polite when we were arguing," Robbie said to Jason. "Maybe we've both learned something about sportsmanship today."

The two boys pulled the mat back where it belonged and turned to tell the trophy good-bye.

"Thanks for a good story," Jason said. "We won't forget about Jim Thorpe."

"Yeah, thanks a lot," Robbie added. "We won't forget about his rules for good sportsmanship either."

With two big grins the best friends waved good-bye to Mr. Trophy and started home.